T0037025

What I saw, heard, learned . . .

GIORGIO AGAMBEN

What I saw, heard, learned . . .

TRANSLATED BY ALTA L. PRICE

LONDON CALCUTTA NEW YORK

This book has been translated thanks to a translation grant awarded by the
Italian Ministry of Foreign Affairs and International Cooperation.

Questo libro è stato tradotto grazie a un contributo alla traduzione assegnato
dal Ministero degli Affari Esteri e della Cooperazione Internazionale italiano.

Seagull Books, 2023

First published in Italian as *Quel che ho visto, udito, appreso . . .*
© Giulio Einaudi editore s.p.a., Torino, 2022

First published in English translation by Seagull Books, 2023
English translation © Alta L. Price, 2023

ISBN 978 1 80309 298 0

British Library Cataloguing-in-Publication Data
A catalogue record for this book is available from the British Library

Typeset by Seagull Books, Calcutta, India
Printed and bound by WordsWorth India, New Delhi, India

CONTENTS

What I saw, heard, learned . . .

At the Church of San Giacomo da l'Orio in Venice, I heard the bells. Of the two ways the devout have chosen to call their people, voice and bell, the latter is so familiar to me that I cannot hear it without a feeling of tenderness. The human voice is too direct and—insofar as it calls upon me, personally—almost indiscreet. Bells, on the other hand, do not ring out with words one needs to understand; they don't call, and they certainly don't call me. They accompany me, enveloping me with their impetuous ring, which then fades so gently—for no reason, precisely as it began. That it is possible to say something without speaking—this is what church bells are to me, this is what I heard at San Giacomo da l'Orio.

In Rome I heard someone say that Earth is the hell of some unknown planet, and that our life is the punishment meted out for their faults on the damned from that other realm. But then what about the sky and the stars and the crickets' singing? Unless we're supposed to think that, in order to make the punishment that much subtler and more atrocious, hell was placed inside paradise.

At Grishneshwar right on the threshold of the temple, I saw a lithe, hesitant, divine nanny goat. After looking at me for a few seconds with a quizzical expression, she quickly moved on.

From Giovanni I learned that one can fall so deeply in love with one's own errors that they become a way of life—but that, in the end, this means that truth will only appear to us as a death wish. And from Bachelard I learned that there is no such thing as original truth, only original error. Truth always comes last, or next to last.

In Scicli I saw that stones are softer than flesh and hay is brighter than the sun. That the Madonna rides on horseback and skewers infidels with her sword. And that, up on the acropolis, the Church of Saint Matthew awaits something that can never come to be.

Everywhere, in every city in the world, I saw that people disparage and accuse one another; and that is why they endure judgement and condemnation with neither respite nor compassion.

From the Gnostic Apelles I learned that knowledge—even knowledge of God—doesn't exist, and if it exists and remains what it is, it's of no importance: the only important thing is 'being moved', the push it gives us.

In Göreme, in the Church of the Buckle, I saw the face of the saint. If you look at it, you cannot help but believe in him. Similarly, there is a word which, if you listen to it, you cannot help but believe to be true.

From Ingeborg I learned that the city we live in is like a language with an ancient, harmonious core surrounded by gas stations, highway interchanges, and horrible suburbs. And that we must resign ourselves to its ugliness just as we accept the terrible language all around us, so that one day, perhaps, we may find the perfect city, the language that has yet to reign supreme. And that is why we cannot know exactly why we live in this particular place or speak this particular language.

One night, along Venice's Zattere, watching the putrid water lap at the city's foundations, I saw that we exist solely in the intermittence of our being, and that what we call *I* is just a shadow continuously bidding farewell and saying hello, barely mindful of its own dissipation. All the machinery of our body serves solely to provide that break, that inversion of breath in which dwells the *I*—the intercessor of its own absence, unforgettable, neither living nor speaking, but the only reason we're given life and language.

From Spinoza I learned that we have two ways of considering things: the way we see them in God, as eternal; and the way we know them in space and time, limited, finite, as if cut off from God. But truly to love someone means seeing them simultaneously in God and in time. The tenderness and shadow of their existing here and now—the amber and crystal of their being in God.

In the coves on the island of Ponza, at Cala Felci, by the Lucia Rosa sea stacks, and at Cala Inferno, I spent a long time looking at the colours— looking at happiness.

In Ajanta, in the half-light surrounding the temple carved into the cliff, I saw the Buddha's face. He was seated in lotus position, teaching. Just as my eyes began to perceive the golden light emanating from the stone, I understood what *contemplation* means, not just stilling the mind, but, along with it, the body. During the instant of contemplation—an eternal instant—you can no longer distinguish between mind and body, and that's what beatitude is.

From the Gospels I learned that people mustn't judge one another, but rather love one another, and that judgement is the punishment they incur every time they stray from love.

From Franco I learned that it's not the 'as if' that is important, but the 'as if not': 'as if we were not Kingdom.' Those who would have us be content with 'salvation as if' are misleading us about the only truth that counts: that we are already Kingdom. 'Since we are not Kingdom,' the moral says, 'we must act as if we were.' The righteous says, instead, that we are Kingdom, but, precisely because of that, we live as if we were not Kingdom, as if He knew of no other path than ours.

In Weimar I saw that Buchenwald is so near that the memory of it gets mixed up with that of Goethe's house and you can no longer distinguish them.

From Anna Maria Ortese I learned that we write in order to escape adult life and rebuild the paradise of childhood. But then, in the end, when we rediscover and recite the nursery rhymes of childhood, we are turned back, bitterly, into adults.

In Venice I saw that people are mummies, and the city is a spectre. So it's more alive than they are—especially at night.

In Le Thor, in 1966, I saw the night sky studded by countless stars. And I promised to remain faithful to it. In that same place, in that same year, I managed to grab onto the last coattail of Western philosophy before it disappeared forever.

In Paris I saw that the most intolerant religion of all is secularism, and that a scarf around the head of a girl can cause greater scandal than the policeman who kills her.

From Indian philosophers I learned that each time it is reincarnated, the soul forgets its previous life. But, when it reaches the last step, and becomes moss, the moss remembers when it was human.

In the necropolises of Tuscia, in the churches carved into Cappadocia's cliffs, and many years before, in Lascaux, I saw that there is a close connection between cave and spirit, even stronger than the connection unifying sky and mind.

Writing, I learned that happiness lies not in poet-izing, but in being poetized by something or someone we cannot know.

In Vienna, one summer many years ago, conversing with a friend, I came to understand that, as important as it is to measure up to the speck of goodness in us all, it is just as important to measure up to our dreck, our abjection. Only the former can give us the strength to accept the latter, but only an understanding of the latter can render the former true.

From infancy: that words are the only thing left from when we were not yet speaking beings. We've lost everything else—but words are the ancestral relics that hold our memory of that time, the little portals through which we can, briefly, return.

From Eriugena, Elijah Del Medigo, Albalag, and Spinoza: that the only reasonable doctrine regarding God is pantheism—which does not mean the inert identity of God and nature, but rather that God makes and modifies himself in things, and things make and modify themselves in God. By creating himself, God creates the world, and by creating the world, God creates himself and 'begins to appear in all his theophanies, everything in everything and everywhere, creator and created, seer and seen, substance and accident . . . creating on every creature and created within every creature', both naturing and natured. And God loses himself in his modes and the modes are lost in God and only this squandering is truly divine—this disappearing, this forgetting of the one in the others and the others in the one.

From Cavafy: that it's not important that the work we leave behind be read and understood. What is important is that one day, someone like us will live and act without obstacle, freely doing what we tried to live and do:

> But maybe it isn't worth so much concern,
> so much effort to discover who I really am.
> Later, in a more perfect society,
> someone else made just like me
> is certain to appear and act freely.

At Alberoni I saw a little girl's face and gesture, both as silent as the angel, and ever since I've been seeking and not seeking to understand. That face surely holds the key to the mystery, but if you try to get your hands on it and turn it, you're lost. On that face, in that gesture, my entire life passed by—impatiently, expectant.

From Mazzarino I learned that one's calling is also one's limit. Where we're most inspired, where we believe we're delving most deeply, is also where we come to know our limit. That is why it's important to question one's vocation and, as soon as possible, to revoke it.

From José Bergamín and the philosophers I love: that comedy is truer than tragedy, and innocence deeper than guilt. From Prince Siddhartha: that guilty action—*karman*—does exist, but not the subject—*ātman*—to which it can be attributed. From Elsa: that if you believe unreservedly in fiction, everything becomes real.

What have I learned from love? That intimacy is something like a political substance, otherwise men wouldn't act as if sharing it were the most precious good in the world. And yet it is excluded from politics and left in the hands of women, who—it appears—seem to know more about it. This is proof that the society we live in is incurably misogynistic and contradictory.

In Paris, in Bonnard's canvases, I saw that colour—which is the form of ecstasy—is also intelligence and constructive reason: contrary to what people usually think, 'line is sensation, colour is reasoning'. Intelligence is not solely a cognitive principle: it is, deep down, something that bestows blessings—or, to give it the same name Dante did, Beatrice—a *Beatrix*. And that is why it can lend form to everything, from a canvas to a life.

From the legends surrounding Homer's death: that the battle between man and language is a battle to the death, that the enigma posed to man by the existence of language cannot be solved. But that it's also ultimately a childish riddle, like the ones fishermen pose to the poet on the seashore.

From Averroes the Andalusian I learned that the intellect is one, though that doesn't mean that everybody thinks the same thing—rather that, when we think the true, the multiplicity of opinions fades and, ultimately, it is no longer I who is thinking. And yet, 'no longer I' means not only that I was there, but that in some sense I still am, because, as Averroes says, I conjoin with the one not through thought—which belongs to the one and not to me—but through the phantasms and desires of the imagination, which is solely mine. And this is also the meaning of Arab architecture: individuals' imaginations are like the variegated ceramic tiles that decorate the walls of the mosque, or like the shimmering light filtering through tiny holes, transcribing a single, complicated arabesque.

From my fellow contemporary Italians I got distraction. There was no attention to be found.

In the mirror I saw that between us and ourselves there is a small gap, a delay that can be measured exactly by the amount of time it takes us to recognize our own image. That minuscule opening gives rise, along with the whole of psychology, to all our neuroses and fears, all the triumphs and failures of the ego. Had we recognized ourselves immediately, had there not been that fleeting intermission, we would be like the angels, entirely devoid of psychology. And we would bereft of the novel, which narrates—this is what psychology is—the time it takes characters to recognize and misrecognize, to avow and disavow, themselves.

From Joachim of Fiore: that the new never comes about through the destruction of the old, because the age to come doesn't annihilate the age that is passing, but rather completes the figure contained therein. And that the ages of the world succeed one another like leaf, stalk and spike.

From my extended periods of idleness: what contemplation contemplates. Not a beyond, where there's nothing to contemplate, nor merely the objects hither, which can only be loved or hated. Contemplation contemplates the sensation within sensation, the mind within the mind, the thought within the thought, the word within the word, the art within art. That is what makes it so happy.

From Bachofen: that myth is the exegesis of a symbol, and that this exegesis can only take place in the form of a story. Our theologians, however, aren't great storytellers; they've turned the tale of Jesus—so fantastic, so light—into a *symbolon*, which to them means a *credo*, that is, a bundle of dogmas.

What water taught me: delight, when our foot no longer finds its hold and our body almost unwillingly gives in and swims.

From Epicurus and Fallot: that what is important about pleasure is only its smallest degree, the one that coincides with the lower limit of sensation, the simple, everyday sensation of existing. To rise each morning with this minuscule joy and hear it softly summoning friendship.

From Lucretius: that the gods live in an in-between world, an interstitial space, and that the good Lord dwells not only in the details but, above all, in the tiny gap that separates each thing from itself. And that the art of living and of becoming divine implies an ability to inhabit not the house, but the threshold, not the centre, but the margin—in other words, to take interest not in holiness but in the halo.

At the opera, listening to Maria Callas, I realized that when we write, the most difficult thing is to sustain a *mezza voce* at the highest register.

In Erik Peterson I read that the Jews, because of their incredulity, delay the coming of the Kingdom. But that means that between Church and Synagogue there is a secret, shady solidarity, because both administer, so to speak, the delay of the Kingdom upon which their existence is founded. As if the Kingdom were a train that could arrive late. It's the exact opposite: the delay—history—is the train from which priests and rabbis do their utmost to prevent us stepping off, to keep us from seeing that we have always already arrived.

What have I learned from poetry? That a political task and a political intensity can be conveyed solely through language, and that this task—although it is thoroughly commonplace—cannot be assigned by anyone, it can only be assumed by the poet in lieu of an absent people. And that nowadays no other possible politics exists, because it is solely through the poetic intensification of language that the absent people—for an instant—appears and comes to the rescue.

From Elsa I also learned that innocence is possible solely as a parody, and that this is also the only possible reparation for our wounded childhood. And that if you make fiction your sole reality, you find certainty, but you lose all hope.

From the places you loved and had to leave: that if, like the fairytale giant, you leave your heart hidden there, sure, you become invulnerable, but you also run the risk of always having to remember—always having to return to the heart you chose to hide there. Which, in turn, will once again make you vulnerable.

From Hugh of Saint Victor: that 'he who finds his homeland sweet is tender, he to whom every soil is like his homeland is strong, and he to whom the entire world is like a state of exile is perfect.' With the proviso that this exile doesn't refer to another, heavenly homeland: rather, as the ancients suggested, exile is the state of he who is alone everywhere or, in keeping with the etymology of the moderns, the condition of he who has found an exit.

From Plato's style: that philosophy needs myth not because the latter is closer to truth, but on the contrary, because myth is indifferent to both truth and falsity. Myth is the antidote to the word's presumption to utter propositions that are solely true (or solely false). If what is at stake in a proposition is the idea, then it is impossible to demand that it be either true or false, as Plato's shrewd disciple was wont to do. The only discourse that is philosophical, Plato suggests, is a discourse that contains its own mythical complement, and can therefore proclaim both 'the truth and falsity of being as a whole'.

From the twentieth century: that I certainly belong to it and I wandered out into the twenty-first only to get a breath of fresh air. But that air was so unbreathable that I immediately turned back—not to the twentieth century, but to a time within time, which I'm not able to place within any chronology, but which is also the only time that now interests me.

From Kafka: that salvation exists, but not for us; that is, we're saved only when we're no longer interested in being saved. It's a lot like when we want to go somewhere at all costs, but then, along the way, walking and living, we forget. If someone tells us we've arrived, we shrug our shoulders as if it had nothing to do with us.

In Ponza I listened to illiterate women recite the Bible in song. They knew the text solely through oral tradition. And I saw that the illiterate are incomparably superior to those who claim to know how to read and write.

From Saint Francis: 'speak and write simply and purely . . . and understand just as simply and without gloss'. We, on the other hand, do nothing but gloss one another.

In Prospero's island: that just as the sorcerer must at some point take leave of Ariel and his spells, so too must the poet eventually bid farewell to his inspiration. Certainly, life thus loses its charm. But the silent angel that takes Ariel's place is called Justice.

In other words, philosophy is a poet's attempt at making inspiration coincide with justice—a task so arduous almost no one succeeds.

From living together: that the existence of the other is an enigma that cannot be resolved; it can only be shared. Sharing this enigma is what humans call love.

What has philosophy taught me? That being human means remembering when we were not yet human, and that man's task is to retain the memory of the not-yet and the no-longer human—the child, the animal, the divine.

From the puppeteer Bruno Leone: that the secret of his art lies in transmitting Pulcinella's voice. But it's not actually a voice, it's just a squat little bobbin covered in thread which the puppet master holds to his palate, where it vibrates like a reed and makes the unmistakable rooster-like crowing children love so much. This means that poetry—that every art—consists in transmitting a voice. But there isn't, in truth, a voice of poetry, because what we refer to as such is really just something you put in your mouth and have to master by using childish little tricks.

In Ginostra a donkey reminded me that, for the ancients, it belonged to the mysteries of Venus, and that donkeys were first and foremost ritual animals: *asinus mysteria vehens*, the mystery-bearing donkey. And that while humans, when faced with mystery, put on airs or collapse, exalt or degrade themselves, being an animal means bearing mystery without any drama—straightforwardly, with just a hint of ruefulness.

Like the dove, we were sent out of the ark to see whether there was anything living left on Earth, even just an olive branch to grasp in our beak— but we didn't find a thing. Nevertheless, we chose not to return to the ark.

What I didn't see, didn't hear, didn't learn . . .

Many years ago, my mother gave me something I had written as a child which she'd kept in a drawer. It unsettled me so deeply that I immediately had to avert my gaze. The page contained a detailed description of what, at the time, clearly seemed to be the secret core of my philosophy. How could the hesitant hand of an eight- or nine-year-old child have managed to identify with such precision the most intimate, involute kernel that all my—his—future books would slowly, strenuously work to unfold? I handed the page back to my mother without a word and haven't seen it since. I don't believe I'll ever be able to find it again, but I know that, with it, my secret was lost. The only recollection I have of it is that it was something like a central void, a suspension or lag of sorts, as if the page had suddenly gone blank. As though, at the core of everything I've tried to experience and write, there were an instant—even a quarter of a second—that remained perfectly empty, perfectly unliveable.

———•———

What had been put into words on that page was so incandescent that I was forced to look away, mentally removing whatever I had read and nearly spelled out with my own lips. Or rather it was as if that boy's own hand—my own hand—had erased right before my eyes whatever had been written, such that all that now remained in my memory was a void, a blank. Why had I pushed that page away in such a hurry? Perhaps out of an unavowable sense of jealousy if, as I believe, it had suddenly, clearly struck me that that childish handwriting had captured on paper the ultimate, unparalleled expression of everything I subsequently tried to say, and that I could never hope to match it.

———•———

What follows is not a reconstruction of that bit of writing—which would of course be impossible—but rather an attempt at reflecting on a double absence. In fact, that lost page contained the memory of another lacuna, the one which my thinking had come to envelop in its growing complication. Everything I had written after that was mere compensation for the oblivion into which that page had fallen, and now it pierced everything I wrote like a hole running right through the middle, marking an immemorial loss in every reminiscence. That imperceptible, lost time was my sole true memory. Perhaps I could draw near to it, but only on the condition—if it was indeed the unsaid that had allowed me to discourse at too great a length—that I somehow leave it unknown: adumbrated yet not clearly defined; revealed yet not proffered. This was, or at least so it now seemed, the only way I might remain faithful to that now legendary piece of writing—the text I had chosen to lose, and for whose absence I now unwittingly blamed myself.

But is it possible—and if so, at what price—for an author to try and grasp his own unsaid? After all, the way in which an author—if we use the term in its Latin sense of 'witness'—allows his unsaid to appear without formulating it undeniably defines the character of everything he does say. Indeed, one could even say that every book has a core, and it's precisely to gain distance from that core—to leave it unsaid and untouched, while somehow bearing witness to it—that it was written. Claiming to grasp something that must remain unuttered means falling from the status of author-witness to assume instead the legal status of author-owner.

This means that precisely what I wanted to think and say was left unthought and unsaid—or only obliquely said—in everything I've written, and that that unliveable quarter of a second is embedded at the very centre of everything I've experienced. And it couldn't have been otherwise. Had

I really tried to cross the threshold of silence that accompanies every thought, I wouldn't have written a thing. What's decisive, in any case, is the ethical relationship the subject has with his unsaid and his unlived, the uncertain limit between what he managed to write and what he could only remain silent about.

———

Every single one of us exists in a state of complication in which everything is enfolded in itself, convoluted, in a way that remains unapparent in every manifestation, unformulated in every word—but we also exist in the casual, completely unconvoluted gesture, in which everything is entirely open and explicated. This is how we're to understand the pantheistic thesis which posits that everything is complicated in God and God unfolds in everything. In every instant, these two realities are contemporary, such that the secret is always exposed in full light and, simultaneously, what has been revealed seems to fall into and almost drown within itself, moving towards an inexplicable centre.

———

These two movements—in God and in us—are in close contact, separated solely by an absence of representation. This is why it's correct to say that there is no secret in either God or us—or, better yet, that the secret is that there is no secret, only a complication that explicates itself and an explication that complicates itself, enfolding inward. At the point of contact—where any and every representation fails—only gladness and splendour remain. But if, as invariably happens, we once again try to represent it—and how could we not?—we fall inward yet again and get all wrapped up in ourselves.

———

Because being loses itself in its modes just as modes lose themselves in being. The point where we seem to explicate ourselves in appearance and move in God, we forget and lose ourselves, just as God, losing himself in us, forgets himself. What is lost belongs to God, and yet, according to legend, Iblīs incessantly grieves what gets lost—as do we along with him.

———

This is why it's rightly been said that, whatever purpose we were created for, we weren't created for success. The fate we've been assigned is failure—in every art and every study, and above all in the chaste art of living well. And yet precisely that—if we manage to comprehend it— is the absolute best that we can do.

———

What I was seeking was precisely this void, this lacunary point of contact between complication and sprezzatura, *exposition and abyss, half-light and splendour—where the secret shows itself in such sharp clarity that it becomes as simple and impenetrable as a childish riddle or a nursery rhyme. This was the central void around which my thinking wrapped itself—the blessed, unliveable lacuna that from the very start, in writing, I couldn't help but leave unformulated.*